TAYLOR'S WORD ON

DEBT

How You Got Into Debt ...

... And How You Can Get Out

MICHELLE TAYLOR

Taylor's Word On Debt

How You Got Into Debt ... And How You'll Get Out

ISBN: 978-1461087847

Order additional copies at www.TaylorsWord.com or with the order form near the end of the book.

Editor
Andrea Daniel

Interior and Cover Design
Tim Miller

Author Photographs
Sudden Utopia Advertising, Design & Photography
www.SuddenUtopia.com

Table of Contents

Acknowledgments

THANK YOU GOD, for your words stand forever (Isaiah 40:8).

Thanks to my parents, Bruce and Barbara Taylor. You two are my greatest inspiration. Thanks for your love, guidance, belief in me and above all, your prayers.

Thank you God for my gift: a heritage from the Lord, the fruit of the womb, my reward, my son Matthew Hall. You bring me happiness, meaning and joy—both sweet and challenging. Thanks for your love.

Thank you Grandma Webb. What can I say? You're the greatest grandmother a granddaughter could ask for. Thanks for your assistance in raising me. Thank you for the prayers that kept our family together. You've shown me not only by your words how to walk in love, but by your actions. Thanks for showing me patience and how to give. May God bless and continue to keep you, Grandma. I aspire to live as long as you've lived and to have a loving spirit like yours through all the days of my life.

To my Grandmother Taylor. Oh how I love, miss and adore you. Even though you've gone on to be with the Lord, I sorely miss you. You are always in my heart and will never be forgotten. I will continue to live out your word to just be nice. I love you.

Special thanks to my family for your love and support: Tasha Johnson, Trust Gordon, Lashawn Sparks, Kimberly Snow, Jessica Taylor, Allison Spencer, Paris McCurdy, Nicole Snow, Jennifer Taylor, Cheri Snow, Dana Hamblin, Nancy Hamblin, Rhonda Hamblin, Jennifer Peeples, Veroneca Travier, Qiana Perry, Deborah Lennon, the Webbs, the Taylors, the Barners, the Matlock and Evans family, the Muhammads, the Gordons and all my aunts and uncles, Auntie Shell's babies, and lastly, a host of cousins..

To my close friends, thanks for the love and words of encouragement: LaCresia Willis, Donald Middleton, Keisha Barksdale, Tasha Carpenter, Felisa Liggons, Leonard Thomas, Janeane Cato, Diana Cannon, Richard Paris, Sam Amir, Alicia Young, Damon Autry, Tanya Rogers, Serena Horton, Robin Griffith, Alisa Davis, Beverly Whitehead, and all my Seneca St. Friends.

Word Of Faith International Christian Center, Fitness Works gym family, Sidney, the best gym instructor ever,

Eric Huffman of State Farm Insurance, Markwei Boye of Smart Business International PLLC, Leonard Thomas Construction, Brick House Designs, Beauty Café, National Realty Centers, New Liberty Baptist Church, New Rising Star, Sylvia Hubbard of the Motown Writer's Network (www.MotownWriters.com), Mark Lang of Wayne County Community College District, Sylvia Clark, author of *Standing on God's Promise*, and Lady Diamond Faith Group Sisters for all of your help and support.

Disclaimer

THIS BOOK IS DESIGNED to provide information on the causes of debt, effects of debt, the importance of setting financial goals and how to maintain a debt-free life. It is presented as a guideline to impart practical information that anyone can use; it is NOT intended to be viewed as a legal source or other professional service. There are experts available who can assist you with those specific concerns.

This text should be used only as a general guide and not as the ultimate source. The purpose of this text is to educate, inspire and motivate. The author and publishing company shall have neither liability nor responsibility to any person or entity with respect to any loss or damage caused, or alleged to have been caused, directly or indirectly, by the information contained in this book.

Introduction

THE EMOTIONAL AND PSYCHOLOGICAL pain was intense. Sleepless nights. Loss of appetite. Deep despair. I often peered at my tattered reflection in the mirror, tears flowing freely down my face. Questions of 'why me?' invaded my every waking moment.

This is a small peek into my psyche while in the midst of a financial calamity unlike any I had ever experienced. A combination of bad decisions, trusting untrustworthy people and a healthy dose of naivety helped contribute to my financial difficulties. The toll it took on my family and me was devastating. I exhausted all options and at the end of the day was left with the painful alternative of filing bankruptcy. While I remain one of about 1.4 million Americans who has filed for bankruptcy in their lifetime, according to the American Bankruptcy Institute, that distinction alone doesn't define me. It's made me wiser and dramatically more understanding of the affects of making ill-advised financial decisions.

But, obviously, I was not always equipped with that understanding. I turned into a student during my experience and absorbed every aspect of financial relevance I could. The result is contained in the following pages, as well as the chronology of how and why I had to file bankruptcy. It is my hope that this information will help you avoid the treacherous pitfalls that I encountered and help you lead a productive life that is devoid of financial restraints.

What Is Debt?

"A life spent making mistakes is not only honorable,
but more useful than a life spent doing nothing."
George Bernard Shaw

THE CONCEPT OF OWING others can be a debilitating
way to live a fulfilling life. Of course we all have some level
of debt throughout our lives, but the life-altering ramifica-
tions occur when that debt becomes an exorbitant amount
that leaves you fighting a no-win battle. The more you pay
the more you seemingly owe. It's a devastating cycle that
can rob you of all the enthusiasm and optimism you enter
each day with. Simply put, Webster's dictionary defines
debt as something that is owed; a state of owing.

At its height, my debt rose to more than $1 million. I
worked for a major telecommunications company in a sales

capacity but was only as good as my previous month's sales. The monthly sales quotas began taking a toll on me, and ultimately I realized that meeting sales quotas mandated by somebody else wasn't what I wanted to do. So I started a real estate investment company in 1999. I purchased homes at low prices and "flipped" them for a profit. In addition to taking out a mortgage on a handful of properties, I incurred additional debt by using my credit cards and bank lines of credit for home improvements and the associated expenses of running a business.

It was not difficult to buy these properties at the beginning. At the time, investors could purchase homes based on "no doc" loans. Banks only required that an investor's banking records reveal a balance that would cover six months worth of payments and a middle credit score of at least 580. My CPA also had to supply a letter stating that he completed my taxes. I easily qualified using those requirements. I also used cash to purchase homes from various auctions, as well as seized properties from the Wayne County Sheriff's department.

So really, it didn't take a lot to buy homes at this time (late 1990s). The real estate market was booming and the seller's market that ensued created a lot of wealthy people. That was my goal. That was my mission. But it didn't quite work out for me like that in the end. I tried selling several inexpensive homes that I had purchased soon after buying them, but I was unable to sale or refinance due to the "seasoning" issue, which states investors must hold properties for six months. In 2008, I purchased a six bedroom investment property for $10,000. I put an additional $25,000 into it for repairs and updates, including a new roof and furnace, new windows, and I updated the electrical system and plumbing. I was told by an appraiser that once the repairs were made the home would be worth $110,000, but six months later that was not the case. By that point, the bank ceased doing no doc conventional loans, plus the property value was worth only $12,000—not the $110,000 the appraiser predicted. That discrepancy was due in large part to the fast-declining real estate market. This was the start of my nightmare because all of my money was soaked into homes that had no value.

This was the case not only with this particular property, but others in my portfolio. Unable to pay the mortgages, I had no choice but to close up shop, wipe the slate clean and start all over. Consequently, I was left to fend for myself in the wake of a growing pile of debt.

There was a time during the late 1990s and early 2000s when the real estate market was booming, but the market plunged several years later to depths unseen in years. By 2008, I found myself owning five homes and owing more than the properties were worth. The total liability was a shade under $900,000, but the value for all five residences was only $374,000.

I had occupants in all of the properties, but the revenue that was generated from my renters was insufficient to cover the inherent expenses that come with property ownership. This left me no other choice but to allow the properties to go into foreclosure. I then began investigating other potential sources of income. I looked into a franchising opportunity with Little Caesar's, as well as a home healthcare business and credit consulting. None of these opportunities ever advanced beyond the dreaming stages because they all required up-front capital—of which I had none. My resources were tied up in my worthless real estate portfolio.

In the end, between outstanding mortgages on five homes, countless credit cards maxed out, and bank lines of credit inching to their limits, I was on the hook for well over $1 million.

Debt Statistics

"If there is any one thing that will bring peace and contentment into the human heart and into the family, it is to live within our means; and if there is any one thing that is grinding and disheartening, it is to have debts and obligations that one cannot meet."

Heber J. Grant

THE STATISTICS REGARDING BANKRUPTCY and debt are sobering reminders that we as a nation are consumed by materialistic gain every moment of our lives. In fact, the 2010 U.S. Census reports that U.S. citizens have more than $886 billion in credit card debt and that figure was expected to rise to more than $1.177 trillion by 2011. Also, U.S. consumers racked up an estimated $51 billion worth of fast food on their personal credit and debit cards in 2006, compared to $33.2 billion the previous year. The average credit card debt per American household is $15,700.

What's more frightening, research shows that one out of 100 households in the United States will file bankruptcy. Studies also show that 43 percent of U.S. families spend more than they earn. According to the U.S. Census Bureau, there were 173 million credit card holders in the United States in 2006 and that number was projected to grow to 181 million by 2011. It is interesting to note that Americans' credit card use is greater than the rest of the entire world combined. The latest statistics from the Federal Reserve indicate that the total amount of consumer debt outstanding remained steady in 2009. The amount of consumer debt in the U.S. stands at nearly $2.5 trillion as of March 2010—that works out to nearly $8,100 for every person living in the U.S. This is just unsecured credit. Further, revolving debt in this country—98 percent of which is made up of credit card debt—totals almost $853 billion as of March 2010.

The Use Of Credit Cards

Using credit cards instead of cash to purchase items keeps us indebted to the credit card companies long after we make the purchase. Insanely high interest rates that in some cases approach 30 percent mean we pay $1.30 for every one dollar we spend. And the compounding effect of high interest rates is what keeps us in financial shackles when it comes to credit card usage.

Many individuals who fall into debt often turn to or rely on credit card relief programs to be their saving grace. But they are often using these types of programs as a "band aide" to heal the problem instead of discovering what the root or main issue really is and work to fix it permanently. Depending on others to help dig you out of a financial hole is only a short-term solution to a life long problem.

If a credit card relief program does not work many are left with the last resort of filing bankruptcy. Bankruptcy, for many, is a label that can last a long time. It's a sign that let's anyone looking to hire or offer you credit know that you are a risk or liability. For some individuals, bankruptcy is a way to start over and try to rebuild what was lost. Because I did not know enough about other options, bankruptcy was the only alternative I thought could remedy my situation. This may be true for some; however I needed to educate myself so I could be equipped to never travel this route again. It is important to learn from your past mistakes so that you avoid them in the future. Only through educating yourself can you ensure that is the case.

More Staggering Statistics

The Federal Reserve reports that Americans charged almost $2 billion to their credit cards in 2006—that's about $11,300 in charges per card holder. This information includes all credit card types. The average interest rate for a standard bank credit card topped 19 percent in 2007, compared to 16.5 percent in 2003.

The average U.S. household pays $950 in interest each year. The National Association of Realtors says the average home owner stays in his/her home a little over seven years, with an eight percent mortgage; the home owner would sell his/her home still owing 90 percent of his mortgage. If this trend continues, the home owner would never pay off the mortgage in his/her lifetime. Only two percent of homes in America are even paid for. These numbers are overwhelming, but they speak to the enormity of the problem regarding the personal financial crisis we face in this country. These facts must be known by all so that their true effects can be fully understood.

My personal unsecured debt amount was just under $400,000—the result of my credit card balances and lines of credit from the bank. Even now my heart sinks when I see that number. But I was determined not to be a statistic. I set out to make a change in my life and rid myself of the emotional and psychological shackles that debt placed on me.

What Does The Bible Say About Debt?

"Keep out of debt and owe no man anything,
except to love one another."

Romans 13:8

RICHARD R. LYMAN, an apostle in The Church of Jesus
Christ of Latter-day Saints, once said *"a man cannot be
comfortable spiritually who is in bondage financially."* I felt
that way. Much of my attention and focus was placed on
my financial situation, leaving little, if any, room for my
spiritual growth. But by reading my Bible, I discovered that
it indeed covers areas concerning debt:

> "But you shall remember the
> Lord your God, for it is he who
> gives you power to get wealth,

that He may establish His cov-
enant which He swore to your
fathers, as it is this day."

Deuteronomy 8:18

"The Lord shall open to you
his good treasury, the heavens,
to give the rain of your land in
its season and to bless all the
work of your hands; and you
shall lend to many nations, but
you shall not borrow."

Deuteronomy 28:12

*"Keep your life free from the love
of money, and be content with
what you have."*

Hebrews 13:5

The Bible warns us against debt. The Bible is against
lenders who abuse those who are bound to them in debt. It
speaks harsh words toward bad lenders, but it does not
condemn the debtor. We Americans have problems and
questions concerning the interest rates charged on loans.

It's mentioned in the Bible that a fair interest rate is expected to be received on borrowed money, (Proverbs 28:8; Leviticus 25:35-38; Matthew 25:27). Debt will make you a slave to the lender.

The Bible teaches us through its wisdom, that it's not a good idea to go into debt. It is wise to seek wisdom where debt is concerned. Nowhere in the Bible is debt listed as sin. But it does advise against reckless borrowing. Proverbs 22:7 states: *"The rich rule over the poor, and the borrower is servant to the lender."* Too much debt can keep us from fulfilling what God created us to do.

Matthew 6:24 states: *"No one can serve two masters, God and money."* Trust in God, not man. God will supply all of our needs according to His riches and glory in Christ Jesus. God provides for us in many ways, but loans were not one of them. When we know better, we are supposed to do better. So why do some of us still struggle with debt?

There's an interesting correlation between what the law says about bankruptcy and what the Bible says about bankruptcy. Bankruptcy, at its core, is about forgiveness of debt. Under U.S. law and under the proper circumstances, debtors can be forgiven of their debt in a Chapter 7 bankruptcy once every eight years. Biblical law says every seven years.

Deuteronomy 15:1-2—"*At the end of every seven years you shall grant a release. And this is the manner of form of the release: every creditor shall release that which he has lent to his neighbor; he shall not exact it of his neighbor, his brother, for the Lord's release is proclaimed.*"

If you have mismanaged your finances, confess your failings to God now. You can receive, by faith, his forgiveness and cleansing (I John 1:9). Remember, there is no condemnation or guilt to those who are in Christ Jesus (Romans 8:1). Jesus, by his love and mercy, gave us a fresh start, a new birth. Bankruptcy, based on the law of mercy with divine origins if necessary, may provide you with a fresh start, a new and brighter economic outlook.

Causes of Debt

"Nothing occurs in your life...which is not first a thought;
thoughts are like magnets drawing effects to you."
Neale Donald Walsh

I HAVE SHARED THE REASONS behind my getting knee-deep in debt. Certainly there are numerous other causes, and here are a few:

❖ **Lack of Money Management** - A monthly budget is essential. Keep track of all of your spending for one week to determine where your money is going. Tracking your expenses may help in finding areas you can eliminate in order to save extra funds.

❖ **Minimized Income** – Sometimes life presents circumstances where our cash flow takes a hit. If that happens, it is imperative to readjust your spending accordingly and not overextend yourselves financially. Reduced income forces you to prioritize and modify your approach.

❖ **Medical Expenses** - Unexpected medical emergencies or illnesses can create a great deal of debt. In fact, medical expenses are one of the leading causes of bankruptcy in America. Maintaining an emergency fund that some experts believe should be three to six months of your annual income is one of the ways to combat this possibility.

❖   **Gambling** - This is an obvious one. Many have lost their homes, their jobs, their savings and their families to this addictive activity.

❖   **Unemployment** - This certainly can result in bills going unpaid due to no income. Another reason why it is important to have an emergency savings fund.

❖   **Divorce** - This has a dramatic impact on finances, especially when lifestyles are based on two incomes.

❖   **Credit Too Soon** - Allowing college students access to credit is a head-scratching business model. Credit card companies and retailers flock to college students and inundate them with insane credit offers. These companies assume that parents will help pay off any incurred debt. Most students have no experience with credit and it is easy for them to charge unnecessarily. This could lead to a pattern of poor financial management in the future.

❖ **No Savings** - Many of us do not save. Saving can help your financial situation when the unexpected happens. Many experts suggest we have three to six months of earnings stashed away in case of emergencies.

❖ **Extravagant Spending** – Keeping up with the Joneses can be the undoing of any rational-thinking person who gets caught up in trying to be something he or she is not. This thinking can lead to a mountain of debt. Proverbs 13:11 says, *wealth (not earned but) won in haste or unjustly or from the production of things for vain or detrimental use (such riches) will dwindle away, but he who gathers little by little will increase (his riches).*

❖   **No Discipline** – Learn to control your impulsive spending habits.

❖   **Fast Money** – This is perhaps better known as attempting to get rich quick. Oftentimes, these tactics don't amount to anything other than heartache and potential financial ruin for those who engage in fast money schemes. There is also a good chance that those who participate in fast money schemes go from one failed attempt to another, further damaging their financial standing—especially with those schemes that require up-front investments. *"A faithful man will be richly blessed, but one eager to get rich will not go unpunished"*—Proverbs 28:20.

Once you accept your true financial situation, you have taken the first step toward financial freedom.

Effects of Debt

"Never take life seriously; nobody gets out alive anyway."
Anonymous

THE EFFECTS OF DEBT can have far-reaching implications that stretch further than you might imagine. I lived that life of financial chaos and it's no fun. My bout with debt wiped me out to the point of insolvency. I had to move back home with my parents; my pride took a hit and my experience broke me down but it didn't break me completely. In fact, it brought me closer to God and caused me to want to use that experience to show others how best to avoid the problems I encountered.

Debt has physical and mental effects on a person's overall well-being—most noticeably a loss of focus at home and at work. Money issues and debt are leading causes of

divorce and marital stress. Research shows that marriages
are most fragile during the first few years, with 20 percent
of divorces occurring within the first five years of marriage
(National Center for Health Statistics, 2001). It is said that
money is one of the topics couples fight about most often
during the newlywed years and a contributing factor in
many divorces. A unique strength of the majority of happily
married couples was that they did not have major debt. Less
debt with couples frees up their time to devote to each
other. According to that same NCHS report from 2001, it
was found that 55 percent of husbands and wives had
automobile debt, 48 percent had credit card debt, 23 percent
had school debt, and 12 percent had medical debt as they
entered marriage.

According to moneymatters101.com, at its worse, debt
can lead to an avalanche of debilitating and potentially
deadly consequences, including foreclosures, wage garnish-
ments, evictions, bankruptcy, emotional break downs, sui-
cides, and in some cases murder. As I mentioned, financial
challenges rob you of your focus and lead you to waste time
giving energy to negativity. Certainly, it's something that
should not be ignored, but looking at the situation from a
different, more positive and upbeat perspective is crucial to
facing and ultimately overcoming one of life's biggest hur-

dles. When you're experiencing debt problems, it's difficult to think about anything else. Debt causes an ungodly amount of stress—as if the weight of the world is sitting on your chest, smothering you and taking your breath away.

Research suggests that stress can bring on or worsen symptoms or diseases. Stress causes anxiety, depression and sleeping problems. According to medical references, 43 percent of all adults suffer adverse health effects from stress, 75 percent to 90 percent of all doctor office visits are for stress-related ailments and complaints. Stress can play a part in problems such as headaches, high blood pressure, heart problems, diabetes, skin conditions, asthma, arthritis, depression and anxiety.

I was mentally paralyzed by my stress. I was an emotional wreck and had headaches every day. In fact, my entire body ached and I had little interest in eating. I tried my best to conceal my feelings by keeping them inside, but sometimes they crept to the surface for all to see.

The stress that's brought on by financial woes in general and debt in particular can be overwhelming, but can be managed. Here are some ways to help cope with this predicament.

Suggestions For Stress Management

❖ Prayer/meditation.

❖ Exercising helps to alleviate stress, so get moving.
(Consult your health care provider before beginning any exercise program.)

❖ Don't keep your problems to yourself. Talk to a professional, religious leader or simply share your feelings and concerns with a friend or close relative.

❖ A healthier diet is essential. Fruits and vegetables can help combat the physical effects that stress can cause.

❖ Sleep. Getting your rest allows the body and the mind to recover. Many professionals recommend seven to eight hours of sleep each night.

❖ Volunteer at your church or one of your favorite charities. These types of activities can redirect your focus off your problems.

Here are sources of help that you can contact if the burden of your problems becomes too much for you to handle on your own:

❖ A mental health center or your state or local health department

❖ A place of worship

❖ The National Mental Health Information Center: www.mentalhealth.samhsa.gov (800) 789-2647

How To Get Out Of Debt

"The significant problems that we face cannot be solved by the same level of thinking that created them."

Albert Einstein

OKAY, SO THE GRIM PICTURE of debt and other financial troubles has been painted. So if you're in debt, how do you get out? Here are a few suggestions:

❖ Seek God for wisdom and guidance.

❖ Dave Ramsey, author, radio host, television personality and motivational speaker, says we should pay the minimum balances on all debt while focusing and paying off the smallest debt first. List all your debts from smallest to largest, excluding your mortgage. If there are two or more items with similar balances, pay particular attention to both the terms and interest rate of each and concentrate on eliminating those with the higher interest rates and least desirable terms first.

❖ Starting a dialogue with your creditors could potentially lessen your obligation. See what the possibilities are of negotiating a settlement option. Understand that your creditors are in business to make money, but if speaking with creditors allows them to receive, say, half of the balance, then it'd be a win-win proposition for you and the creditors. Of course, the best plan of all as far as getting out of credit card debt is to avoid it altogether. This may not be an option for everyone, however.

❖ Keep track of your expenses. A budget can help you stick with your plan. This method is part of identifying your barriers, your limitations—what you can do financially. Financial advisors say that making a household budget and sticking to it helps create the discipline necessary to make significant progress.

❖ Ridding yourself of credit cards is yet another way to help get you out of debt. Whipping out a small, worthless piece of plastic to pay for an item seems like an innocent thing to do. But once you realize that using that credit card means potentially paying three times what the original cost is because of ridiculous interest rates, you may start thinking twice about using it. Practicing this step, though, will surely put you on the right track toward eliminating your debt.

❖ Attend a seminar about financial literacy. Understanding how money works, at its core, will give you greater comprehension and ultimately greater comfort when it comes to your own financial circumstances.

❖ Talk to or work with a financial advisor. Soliciting advice from an industry professional can help guide your decisions regarding what to do with any extra funds you may have at the end of the month.

❖ Transfer your balance from one high interest creditor to one with a lower interest rate. This helps pay off debt much sooner.

Finding myself with a seven-figure liability caused me unspeakable stress. But I dedicated every day to getting myself out of that dark psychological hole and used every option at my disposal.

One option that I chose was filing bankruptcy. I'm not a proponent of filing bankruptcy every time financial turmoil enters our lives, but sometimes our circumstances leave us no choice. I acknowledged my mistakes and decided to live with and accept the consequences of those misguided decisions by filing bankruptcy.

Earning Extra Income

Find creative ways to earn extra income to help eliminate debt. Here are some ideas:

- ❖ We're all good at something. Why not use your skills to make extra money? Honestly, what better way to earn extra income than by doing something you probably already do for free? Take advantage of your talent and make a couple extra bucks in the process.

❖ Have a garage sell to earn extra cash and rid yourself of those gently-used items that have been piling up.

❖ Find a second part time job.

❖ Ask your employer for a raise. Remember to be tactful and share with your boss the value that you bring to the company. Always give them a reason why your role is vital to the success of the business.

❖ Become a Realtor. We all need a place to live, right? People will always be in need of shelter, so why not be the point person for them? Indeed, it is a competitive industry, but keep in mind that the competition seems to wane during slow markets. Also remember that there's generally a small upfront investment and continued costs associated with being a Realtor, but the profitability can be huge in this field. Plus, you can get started while you're working a full-time job.

❖ Become a paid participant as part of a focus group or even a secret shopper.

Saving Money

"A penny saved is a penny earned."

Benjamin Franklin

Saving money in practical ways is also another way to increase discretionary cash flow. Here are some suggestions:

❖ Cell phones have quickly taken the place of land lines at home. Eliminating your home phone could, in some cases save you as much as $100 per month.

❖ If basic cell phone usage is all you need, think about ridding your contract of all the bells and whistles you're paying for, but not using. Internet service, unlimited text messaging, picture mail—all those features are not necessarily needed for those looking for simple and practical—and less expensive—uses of their cell phone.

❖ Smoking and drinking alcohol can do more than jeopardize your health. They can wreck havoc on your budget. Eliminating these habits can save you a bundle of cash.

❖ You may be able to find savings with your car insurance, home owners insurance or renters insurance. Doing a little investigative analysis can prove to be an effective way to find savings. You can also look into increasing your deductible. Generally speaking, the higher the deductible, the lower the monthly payment.

❖ Eliminate paying for certain services at home. If you pay for a lawn cutting or snow removal service, consider performing those chores yourself. Obviously, if you're physically unable to do it yourself, paying others is the best alternative.

❖ Instead of going out to lunch every day with coworkers, why not bring your lunch from home? Doing so could save you at least $7 a day, or $140 a month.

❖ Going to the movies is entertaining, but it can be an expensive outing. Instead of going on a Saturday night, attend a matinee and see the same movie. Some matinee prices can be as much as half off the price you would pay on a Saturday night.

❖ Coupons can be your best friend when grocery shopping for the family. Don't ignore those circulars. They could save you tons of cash.

❖ Instead of that $3 coffee, why not enjoy a $1 bottle of water instead? Better yet, drink FREE water from home.

❖ Eat out less often.

The Importance Of Setting Financial Goals

"Our goals can only be reached through a vehicle of a plan,

in which we must fervently believe, and upon which

we must vigorously act. There is no other route to success. "

Stephen A. Brennan

SOME AMERICANS SPEND MORE time planning a summer vacation than they do certain aspects of their financial lives. That's a sobering fact indeed, and one that highlights the need for us to put into better focus the financial viability of our lives.

For starters, learning to set financial goals at an early age, (ages 11-18) can lead to a secure and successful financial background that will remain stable and constant.

Most children receive allowance for doing simple chores around the house. Usually, the child saves the money to buy a special treat. This child is setting a goal and habits that he/she will probably maintain through adulthood. Everyone should set goals and try to achieve them; regardless of how small, i.e. get a car wash by Tuesday at 11am; or how grand, such as buying a home by February 28, 2014). Small steps lead to giant strides.

Set your goals and make them attainable. The bible scripture James 2:20 says, "Faith without works is dead"; so is a goal without an action. Without a goal or a plan in place, you're just living. A goal can be to lose weight, increase your income or go back to school. Here are some suggestions to take into account when setting goals—financial or otherwise.

❖ Write down your goals; short-term and long-term. Make sure your goals are obtainable. Remember that several small steps can lead to giant strides.

❖ Have your goals in a place where you can view them daily. Keeping your goals within sight will help you keep your focus and work towards accomplishing them.

❖ Give your goals a realistic timeframe. Six months, two years or five. By doing this, you hold yourself accountable and have something to work toward.

❖ Your goals should be prioritized. Some goals may take many years to reach, while others could be day-to-day options. Whichever it is, pursue the most important, the most time-sensitive goal first

before moving on to the next
one.

❖ Your goals are not set in stone,
so if changes are needed, make
the changes necessary to complete them. Sometimes circumstances arise that halt your
progress. Do not fret just keep
pressing towards the mark.

❖ Share your goals and opinions
with those around you whom
you trust. These allies can act
as cheerleaders and motiva-
tors.

Goal-setting strategies should include setting and sticking to a budget. Here are a few simple suggestions on how
to establish a budget:

How To Create A Budget

❖ List your monthly income and monthly expenses.

❖ Subtract your monthly income from your monthly expenses. Kudos to you if your income exceeds your expenses; if not, the next step is important.

❖ Examine your monthly expenses. What's fluff, what can be eliminated, what's discretionary? Scrub your list and see if you can free up extra cash by being diligent and honest with yourself and your true needs.

Everyone should have a budget and creating one is not a hard or scary task. With today's fast paced technology and software programs, many tools are available to help create and manage, as well as, update your budget on the computer. If you don't have a computer or are not very skilled at using a computer, using paper and a pen will be just as effective. If you choose to create your budget the old fashion way, start by writing down what you bring home, them start deducting:

Deductions

- Tithes – 10 percent
- Pay yourself 10 percent. If you don't give yourself a reward, chances are you won't stick with the plan.
- Savings or investments (emergency fund)
- Mortgage/rent
- Utilities
- Car Note
- Food
- Debt obligations
- Cell phone bills

- Cable
- Other:
  - *Dining out*
  - *Entertainment*
  - *Hair appointment*
  - *Shopping*

The number you come up with should then be subtracted from your net income. Having a positive number gives you greater flexibility when it comes to deciding what to do with what's left. Pay off debt, save or invest.

If you arrive at a negative number, find an area or two that may provide you with some wiggle room. Reviewing your list could help you discover hidden dollars where you once thought none existed.

Take your budget seriously. Once you have your budget in place, stick to it. Keep tabs on your budget and make changes where and when needed.

Your spending may change monthly. Expenses may occur outside of the norm. Staying on top of your budget plan will help with your savings and debt elimination goals.

Plus it helps if there are ever any unexpected expenses.

To achieve your goals, it takes commitment, motivation and discipline and action. These actions are best instituted when following a sound plan—namely creating a solid road map for your financial life. It's sort of like developing a business plan. Businesses of all sizes use this practical document and often refer to it when it seems business has veered off course. The same approach can be taken in our personal lives. While it may be painful to view your circumstance on paper, it is a necessary step in coming to grips with and, ultimately fixing our financial situation.

You Received A Huge Sum Of Money . . . Now What?

Imagine if a family member left you hundreds of thousands of dollars. What would you do with it? Receiving a large sum of unexpected money can certainly be an exciting experience. The first thing to do in that instance is take control of your emotions. It would be easy to allow emotions and impulses to override your common sense. But getting the proper professional guidance should be job #1. A highly-seasoned financial advisor can assist you with setting up both short and long-term strategies to ensure a proper future for yourself and your family.

This would also be a good time to seek God for wisdom. People would come out the woodwork trying to get a piece of your money. But trusting in God's guidance will surely help lead you down the path toward financial enlightenment while being a blessing to those around you. And with all that surplus of money, eliminating your debt obviously becomes an easier task.

Do wealthy people have fewer financial problems than those less well off? That's not always the case. It's never really about how much we make; rather, it's about how much we save. Many people increase their standard of living as their income increases. That's a strategy that's bound to keep you a financial prisoner. It's crucial that we develop the knowledge of having our money work for us. That can be done by partnering with a financial professional, by reading books, attending seminars, or any number of other activities.

We hear far too often the tales of Hollywood stars or professional athletes who encounter financial difficulties soon after walking away from the spotlight. Certainly, they have no shortage of advisors surrounding them for probably every aspect of their life, so how do they end up in financial ruin? Surely, most of it has to do with foolish spending. Hairdos costing hundreds of dollars several times a week, garages full of $100,000 European automobiles, jewelry worth as much as houses—it's amazing. These are all one-way tickets to serious financial issues—if, of course, the proper attention isn't paid to what's happening. I am not implying that every wealthy person who splurges on those items is doomed for failure; I am simply pointing out the possibilities of such an occurrence should they lose focus.

How Interest Works FOR You: The Rule of 72

The Rule of 72 may be something most people are not aware of, but knowledgeable investors certainly are. The Rule of 72 is one of those weird mathematical quirks that can actually predict how long it would take your money to double. The rule is simple to apply. Just take the number 72 and divide it by the interest you're earning on your money. For example, if you invest a lump sum of $2,500 and you earn six percent interest, it would take 12 years for your money to double. That number is determined by dividing 72 by six, giving us the 12-year time frame.

How Interest Works AGAINST You

I referenced earlier the potential for paying triple the price for an item if you use a credit card. Here's how that works. Let's say you charge $2,500 worth of home audio and video equipment to your credit card that charges 19 percent interest. That 19 percent interest is what's called the annual percentage rate, or APR, and spread out over a year's time means you pay about 1.59 percent interest per month on the balance.

Let's also assume you are making the minimum payment due each month of $50. The 1.59 percent monthly interest is charged to you, meaning in interest alone you are paying $39.75. The remaining $10.25 goes toward the $2,500 principal. How long would it take you to pay off a $2,500 liability by paying $10/month? You get the picture. Too long.

How To Avoid Debt Altogether

"Keep out of debt and owe no man anything,

except to love one another."

Romans 13:8

HINDSIGHT BEING WHAT IT IS, I certainly would have done many things differently to avoid the chaos and mayhem I encountered. I would save more capital and rely very little—if at all—on credit cards. I had a bad habit of taking care of other responsibilities before taking care of myself, so I would certainly make it a point to pay myself first.

Paying tithes is an essential part of maintaining a sturdy financial regimen as well. I neglected to do that when in the midst of my turmoil. Here are a few other ideas that could prevent you from encountering debt:

- ❖ Seek wisdom from God. The book of Proverbs in the Holy Bible is an excellent start.

- ❖ Talk to a trusted financial adviser.

- ❖ Stick to your budget/track your spending.

- ❖ Put your needs ahead of your desires.

- ❖ Use cash instead of credit cards.

- ❖ Stay away from cash advances.

- ❖ Avoid taking out a second mortgage.

❖ Control your shopping habits.

❖ Buy what you can afford.

❖ Establish an emergency fund to prevent the use of credit cards in the event of an unforeseen situation.

❖ Live within your means.

How To Maintain
A Debt-Free Life

"So do not worry or be anxious about tomorrow,

for tomorrow will have worries and anxieties of its own."

Matthew 6:34

WE'VE GONE OVER THESE IDEAS earlier, but the importance of avoiding debt altogether bears repeating. Here are some ideas:

❖ Keep a record of your finances (what's coming in, what's going out).

❖ Create an emergency fund

that's three to six times your monthly income.

❖ Reserve the need to borrow money only in extreme circumstances.

❖ Control your spending.

❖ Seek professional advice and guidance.

❖ Dedicate yourself to a budget.

❖ Make your money work for you, not the other way around.

The Joy Of Being Debt Free

❖ healthier relationships and lifestyle

❖ more time to spend with family

❖ no more worrying over financial troubles

❖ disposable income available for
   retirement, vacations, etc.

❖ a happier you

❖ freedom.

There's something emotional and psychological about
using a credit card vs. cash. Whipping out a credit card to
make a purchase has a strange feeling of perhaps getting
something for free. The appeal of that small, plastic, worthless card is intoxicating. *Why pay for it now when I can get
what I want and pay for it later* is the feeling that using a
credit card promotes. I know, that mindset had me trapped.

Cash, on the other hand, is immediate. You get what
you want and pay for it now. I'm certainly not suggesting
that using cash prevents individuals from experiencing debt.

I'm simply saying that credit card usage is a potentially dangerous game with significant and long-lasting consequences. Think before you use that card. And all things being equal, use cash instead.

Testimonials

"Life consists of what a man is thinking of all day."

Ralph Waldo Emerson

BRENDA CRAWFORD, AGE 64, retired IRS worker, up to her ears in debt. When asked, how does debt make her feel, she replied, "I feel confined and paralyzed." She explained that she obtained the debt by using credit to help raise her family and pay other bills when she fell short of cash. She's now taking steps to get out of debt by paying a little above minimum payments and paying timely to avoid late fees. When asked if she would do it all again, she stated, "I would use better and wiser choices."

Belinda Thomas, age 50, U.S. postal employee of 20 years. She feels terrible, angry and depressed at times. "I'm angry because I should never have allowed myself to get into debt," which happened by helping others. She was happy about being able to receive credit. "But I went overboard with it." She stated that credit card companies are liars and legal pimps. "They say 'fixed rates,' but after awhile, everything changes." Debt has caused her headaches, diabetes and arthritis. "I'm doubling up on my payments to try to get out of debt. [If I had it to do over again] I would have paid cash instead of using credit cards."

Leonard Thomas, age 44, automotive manufacturer employee for 14 years, entrepreneur for 22 years. He is currently in debt with a mortgage and credit cards. "Debt is depressing to me only when I fall behind. I wouldn't be in debt if I hadn't helped others." He's doing a short sell on his home and plans to pay off his credit card debt within 60 days.

Bruce Taylor, age 60, retired sheet metal worker, states he is not in debt. He had a credit card at the age of 20 for $1,000 and hasn't had one since. He sees no need to get credit, and feels cash is king. "I like to write checks instead of using cash. I've been doing this for 30 years," which has allowed him to successfully track his spending the entire time. His advice is, "Stay out of debt and live within your means."

Steve Rodgers, age 47, assistant manager for 21 years, is in debt. "Debt makes me feel uncomfortable and seems like a form of bondage." Rogers borrowed more than he had to pay back in a 30- day period. He got into debt for personal and family reasons when he needed assistance to acquire things for his family. He's been educating himself on how to eliminate his debts. "I've always paid my bills on time. My advice is to pay as you go in life and save to get what you want using cash." He feels it's okay to obtain debt for a house or car.

Nettie Webb, age 87, retired from American Red Cross in 1987. "I've been in debt since I've been in the world and I'll be in debt until I leave," she says. Her source of debt stems from an equity line from her home and her credit cards.

"I'm in debt because I don't have any money and have to use credit for my day-to-day expenses." Her advice to young people is never go beyond what you can afford to pay.

Susan Rosanski, age 40, administrative assistant for 21 years, is in debt due to credit cards, student loans and a car loan. She's been in debt for over 10 years. "Debt makes me feel like I'm suffocating, not free, pressured—like my money isn't my money." She's checking scriptures on money and seeking the help of God. She's also taking financial classes and implementing what she's learning. Her advice is to pay your tithes, offerings and yourself first. "Work for you; invest in yourself; delay your gratifications."

Startling Facts

❖ Many people are not aware that credit card companies don't only review your credit worthiness before they issue a credit card to you. They also routinely review your information once your credit has been established with them. This is a standard operating procedure that is commonplace in the industry. And depending on what they uncover, they could actually adjust your interest rate or modify your credit limit. As always, if there are questions that arise from changes to your relationship with your creditors, do not hesitate to contact them.

❖ Way too many fees. Next to insanely high interest rates, fees are a creditor's best friend. Annual fees, late fees, membership fees, over-the-phone payment fees, copy of statement courtesy fees, check bounce fees, forget to sign a check fees and ATM fees are all ways that can drain our pockets and bank accounts before we even know what hit us.

❖ Consumers who become the unfortunate targets of collection agencies should know that there's only a certain amount of time that those companies can contact them. This window of time is different from state to state. Once the time to contact you elapses, the debt, for all practical purposes, is no longer collectible. This fact should be shared with the collection agencies, along with following up with something in writing to them stating the expiration of the statute of limitations.

❖ This particular fact is not very well known. Some consumers have even taken a step toward informing creditors of their financial state—to the extent, in some cases, of providing creditors with a thorough breakdown of their cash flow. This financial balance sheet essentially acts as a budget and identifies a consumer's financial obligations, as well as their ability (or inability) to contribute to paying off the debt.

Understanding Your Credit Score

❖ Most of us pay our credit card bills in a timely fashion. This practice is especially important if those credit cards have high interest rates. If you do find yourself the owner of a high interest credit card, but you have a solid payment history, inquire about the possibility of having the credit card company lower your interest rate. Credit card companies, even with their tendency to sometimes do things that go against consumers' best interests, are often known to adjust rates simply by asking. Give it a try.

❖ Your credit score follows you wherever you go. But how is this number determined? It's actually a ridiculously complex formula that's utilized to come

up with your credit score between 300-850. The Fair Isaac
Corporation (FICO) actually
created the software for deter-
mining credit scores. It may
seem as though the industry
purposely employed a convo-
luted formula to confuse the
public. But whatever the case,
be sure to keep your score as
high as possible (preferably
anything over 720).

❖ The strength of your credit
ranking is a key component in
your quality of life. It not only
affects your ability to receive
goods and services on credit,
but it can also influence whether or not we can rent an apart-
ment, obtain affordable

insurance or get a promotion at work.

❖ You have the right to work out arrangements with a collection agency regarding your delinquent account. You can often work out favorable terms. Keep in mind, too, that you should negotiate your terms FIRST before paying the bill. You should also be sure to receive something in writing from the credit card company that reflects the agreed-upon terms of the repayment. This kind of agreement could have a positive impact on your credit score.

❖ If filing bankruptcy proves to
   be a last resort for you, apply
   for a secured credit card. This
   is a good start to rebuilding
   your credit. This is borrowing
   from your own money and it
   will help to rebuild your score.
   Be sure to review and fully understand the terms and conditions on these cards. Fees for
   secured credit cards can be a
   deterrent to some people.

About.com shares how good credit is based on 5 com-
ponents:

• how much you owe: 30 percent

• credit mixture (house, car.
   credit card, etc.): 10 percent.
   (This could help to boost your

score.)

- length of credit history: 15 percent

- how you pay: 35 percent

- new credit inquiries: 10 per-cent.

How To Maintain Good Credit

❖ On-time monthly payment is key.

❖ If at all possible, pay as much as you can.

❖ Keep the accounts open that are in good standing.

❖ Try to maintain a balance that stays below 30 percent of your credit limit.

❖ Keep inquiries into your credit history to a minimum. These inquiries have a negative impact on your score, as they can decrease your score two to four points. These inquiries remain on your credit report for two years.

In the event that negative information is included on your credit report, remember that it is only allowed to remain for a certain period of time. Note for following:

- Late payments: seven years from the date of original delinquency

- Civil suits and civil judgments: seven years from filing date

- Collection agency accounts: seven years

- Paid tax liens: seven years

- Bankruptcies: ten years from the settlement date

Taylor's Word On Debt

DEBT CAN BE A demoralizing and life-stalling experience. When in the midst of it, debt can feel like bondage. You feel limited, stuck, unable to breathe, to function the way you would like. Why put yourself through that? There is no enjoyment, peace or happiness when you owe someone. And I'm not referring to owing a close friend a couple hundred dollars. I'm referring to owing credit card companies and other debt sources large sums of money where a ridiculous amount of interest is accrued.

I remember during my freshman year in college, a JCPenney representative was on campus offering students credit cards. Most of us didn't have jobs, were fresh out of high school and had no knowledge of how to even use the card. "You're approved," the rep said. Me...approved? How exciting. *What did 'approved' mean?* I thought to myself. I really didn't know and quite frankly didn't care. It sounded as if things would be free. The rep indicated I was approved for $300 dollars. Three hundred dollars of free money to a broke college kid sounded good to me. I was ready to run to the nearest JCPenney store the same day. The rep told me the card would arrive within the next seven to 10 days. The card arrived at my parents' home a week later as promised. When I arrived home that following week to visit my parents, my dad informed me that he cut up my card and said that I was not allowed to have a credit card. What do you think I did next? What any other hardhead teenager would have done: I immediately called to get a replacement card mailed to my dorm room. I used up the entire amount of credit in one day once I received the new card. My dad found out later when a statement was sent to my parents' address by mistake. Needless to say my dad was furious.

This was just the beginning of my troubles with debt. My dad refused to pay any of the JCPenney bills and before

I knew it I had created bad debt for myself and ruined my credit before I could even get started. Without a job or means to pay my debt, within a few years my $300 bill turned into $700. My account went delinquent and my credit was shot. I didn't understand the process of credit or debt, so I didn't care. After five years I received a call from a bill collector while I was at my grandmother's house. What a coincidence. I just came over to visit. I remembered that I put my grandmother's number down as a second contact number on my credit application with JCPenney. The bill collector was yelling at me and threatening to have my wages garnished. Although I was 23 years old at the time, that call frightened me. I was offered a settlement amount to avoid further action. I took it happily.

This is where it all began for me. Eighteen years old. How sad. Most 18-year-olds are still dependent on their parents, so why is it okay for credit card companies and retailers to think that teen-agers are wise enough to make credit decisions that can potentially affect their lives before they even start a career? All the credit card companies care about is the money. I believe that credit and money management should be required courses in high school. But beyond that, let's go back to the days of saving and instill that in our children at an early age.

My situation regarding debt caused me great pain and I became paralyzed with fear, regret and anxiety. My thoughts were constantly on figuring out a way to get myself out of this mess I created. Deep depression came over me. I thought of how my situation with debt would hurt and affect so many of my loved ones. My naivety, my pride—which is a sin—and lack of knowledge got me into this situation.

My whole experience with debt caused things to crumble around me. I lost my home, moved in with my parents and had no job at the age of 40. What was I going to do? My answer was church. I attended church three days a week. I studied the Bible every day. Everything that was happening caused me to humble myself completely. I realized that my situation was due to leaning on to my own understanding; listening to others who didn't know any better. I learned through my studies in the good book to give all of my cares, concerns and worries to God. Repent of my wrong and trust God, going forward in all things.

When I gave my situation to God I noticed peace and joy in my life again. Instead of being embarrassed about moving back home, I started being thankful that I had parents to go back home to. Standing on my faith kept my focus off of what I was lacking and brought me to a place where I was able to move forward and not allow my joy to be robbed from me. I learned to turn my mess into my message through this book in hopes of inspiring and helping others realize that it's not just them—that they are not in this alone. Whatever challenges we face, we can and will get through them. I realized that my faith was all I needed.

Why are we here? I've read all kinds of get rich books, heard quite a few motivational CDs and heard many motivational speakers. Everything I heard and read was positive and encouraging. But if I don't utilize the tools correctly, it's worthless. Once I began to seek God and truly have a relationship with the Creator through prayer and study, I realized why I was here. That's when I realized the concept of 'why not me?' It's not about Michelle and what Michelle wants.

The bible teaches that we're here to share God's good news, to appreciate life, our freedom, to let go of doing it ourselves and allow the Creator to help us. Trouble will not last long if we keep the faith. We have to learn to not let our circumstance or situation steal our joy. You've read what worry, fear and anxiety can do to our bodies. We have to learn to stay positive no matter what it looks like. Our thoughts, whether negative or positive, determine the outcome of our future. Stay positive and know that we are all sinners saved by God's grace. Let's seek God for wisdom, and let's educate ourselves and our children. Be mindful of our thoughts. Once you seek wisdom and stand on faith and not allow your circumstances to paralyze you or rob you of your joy, victory will be inevitable.

The Creator gives us a second chance. It's not over until God says it's over. Positive thoughts give way to positive lives and negative thoughts give way to negative lives. A positive mind gives way to faith and trust, while a negative mind gives way to fear and distrust. Don't allow your past pain to cause you to doubt or waiver on your faith. Proverbs 23:7 states that "for as he thinks in his heart, so is he." To feel guilty, depressed or sad is not freedom. It's time we stop complaining and be thankful.

In my search for wisdom to get out of my situation, I often read Joyce Meyers' amplified bible, which asks questions that touched home with me, and they may touch home with you, too: Have you reached the point in your life where you are tired of trying to figure things out on your own? Are you willing to let go and let God? To me this means, you must be willing to ask for help. Repent of sin, ask God to come into your heart and let go and give it all to Him. Let the Creator know that you can't live this life without Him. Surrender it all to Him completely and place your trust in Him. Once you do that you will experience peace. Peace in our hearts gives us true confirmation that we are trusting in God.

Have you ever been in a situation and you knew you should not do something because of limited income? Or have you gone somewhere you should not have gone and you were left with regrets because you did not listen to your "gut" guiding you in the right direction? Well, the gut feeling is not a feeling of peace and if you ever feel like this, stop before moving forward. If there is no peace, there will be panic. Remember the old saying, "Go with God", because "if God is for us, who can be against us?" (Romans 8:30.)

After people fall into difficult situations, such as debt, instead of admitting fault and/or seeking help, they try to work out the problem without seeking strong Godly counsel or financial advice. They, actually make the "hole" they are in deeper and wider. They let pride get the best of them and they fall short of their victory. According to Joyce Myer's Amplified bible, "Pride is a self-absorbed mental state masquerading as confidence. Pride limits our ability to live a free productive life. Do away with pride because it keeps us from obtaining the promise of God".

Why are so many people unhappy with their lives? The world is full of people who are looking for love, comfort, peace, contentment, joy, satisfaction, relationships, children or material things to fill a void. Looking to fill a void through things or people never works. When things or people don't work in our favor, depression, anger, hatred, resentment and bitterness begin to manifest within our spirit. Some start depending on substances like drugs, alcohol or other crude devices. What's sad is people waste a lot of time, energy and their lives searching for some satisfaction in things that are insignificant. They never find the joy of realizing the one they really need. God does not want us to place anyone or anything before him. That's why when we try, we end up frustrated. Relationships, money and children are all gifts from God to be appreciated but not to be a substitute for God's love. Once you place Him first in your life in everything you do, you will be happy and fulfilled.

Making an investment in God is the best investment you can make for you and your loved ones. Psalm 30:3 says, "O Lord, you have bought my life up from Sheol (the place of the dead) you have kept me alive, that I would not go down to the pit." Be blessed and take strength in knowing you can overcome debt, and with God on your side all things are possible.

Why Me?

PEOPLE OFTEN ASK 'WHY ME?' when they encounter challenges and difficult circumstances in their life. But I've learned to flip it and ask 'why _not_ me?' It was George Bernard Shaw who stated "a life spent making mistakes is not only honorable, but more useful than a life spent doing nothing." And that's how I now view my shortcomings: as unfortunate missteps experienced while pursuing a more active, more fruitful and more multi-faceted life. Romans 2:11 of the New International Bible, says God does not show favoritism. We all fall short and no man is perfect. I stopped focusing on how I got here and began focusing on moving forward. I trust that God will continue guiding me in the right direction while leading me to freedom and victory.

In solving my debt problem, I have turned the channel of my thoughts by setting goals for my future and fine-tuning my budget. I am keeping my mind focused on the solution by being of service and helping others, and by working on different projects for income to maintain a healthy surplus of financial resources. There's light at the end of this dark tunnel I entered in 2008. I no longer allow debt to paralyze me or consume my every waking moment. Life is too short and I want to live free from bondage.

Why me? Well, why NOT me? I was raised to always do what's right, treat others the way I want to be treated and have integrity. My grandmother instilled in her children and grandchildren to be nice. I equate that to God, who is love. My character is one based on trust, loyalty and dependability. I look to the good in people first until they show otherwise. I can show trust and loyalty to people who may not be deserving of my trust. I was raised by two great parents who introduced me to Christ at a young age and taught me morals and great work ethics. Both my grandmothers, Mrs. Cathleen Taylor and Mrs. Nettie Webb, gave me wisdom, the importance of staying humble and giving God the glory and praise for every blessing. My greatest gift from God is my son. It was tough raising my son as a single mom. His dad and I left college and married pretty young. My marriage didn't last long and I never wanted to be a statistic as a single mom, but it happens to the best of us.

I strive to be a righteous person, and I treat others with respect and kindness. I have morals and integrity and support from family and friends. So how did I end up in so much debt? How did I end up in this mess? These questions often crossed my mind while going through a deep depression caused by the mental and psychological strain of my financial situation. My entire family was proud of the success I had enjoyed prior to my financial situation. They didn't know that behind my smile and joyous external appearance was a person inside crying out for help. How could I tell my parents about my situation? It would break their hearts. I had it made being raised with both my parents at home as an only child. My dad worked until he retired in 2010. My mom is still working and has been with the same company since 1981. I am truly blessed to have been raised in a stable household. There were never shutoff notices or bill collectors ringing the telephone or knocking on the door. My parents have resided in the same home since 1974.

I am a go-getter by nature. I have always been the

self-motivated type. I always wanted to strive to be the best and give the best to my son. It was my goal by the time my son finished middle school, to move him into a city I thought would provide the best education. I wanted to move him into a culturally mixed school so that going away to college wouldn't be a culture shock, like it was for me. Things were going well until the economy tanked. I then began trusting man instead of God. The whole year of 2010 was a year of change and rearrange in my life. It was funny that my Bishop spoke of the year of change and rearrange at our 2010 New Year's Eve service. He couldn't have been more on point because I was definitely feeling the change. I lost everything—home, money, pride and even friends I thought cared about me. But once things hit bottom for me, those friends vanished into thin air.

God started moving people and things from my life that meant me no good. He wanted me all to himself. I didn't realize how my life was so out of order. I was busy focusing on material things and people instead of God. I had to have them stripped from me to see the true light, which is the love of people, giving and putting God first.

There were days when I didn't want to get out of bed during my depression. And when I did, the strain was clearly etched on my face. My shoulders drooped, my demeanor took a 180-degree turn, my temper was quick. My mom would often ask what was wrong and my eyes would immediately swell with tears. I couldn't dare let her know. I felt so defeated. I became stronger, however, after blowing the dust off my bible. Going back to church regularly and seeking the word of God helped the shame and despair and depression fall off my back. I knew that God would never leave me nor forsake me. I realized more that God was the one supplying my daily needs. I came to know that the joy of the Lord was my strength and how he was the creator of all things. That was where I found my strength. You must find yours. I began to take my focus off of my problem of debt and turned my focus to the solution and possibilities of debt freedom. I encourage you to move toward hope and victory by changing your focus.

We must remember that God gives us new mercy and grace every day and never puts more on us than we can handle. You cannot have a testimony without going through a test. Our experiences—good or bad—are someone else's gain. When our process is complete, someone else is going through that same test. Your message of how you made it to victory can help and encourage another person. I had to realize that every test and trial has a season to help us grow and to help others. I consider myself blessed in overcoming guilt, shame, fear, and self-pity. Look at your debt problem and how you got there in a different light. See how you can use your life experiences and turn them into someone else's gain. Can your past mess help relieve someone else's stress?

This is the reason I wrote this book. I have tried to put everything on the line by being open and honest about my past lessons. Remember, every test and trial has a season and 2008-2010 was my season. I claim a breakthrough, victory and restoration for the future. Name and claim yours.

Helpful Resources

CREDIT COUNSELING: National Foundation for Credit Counseling (NFCC); call 800-388-2227 or www.nfcc.org

RECOMMENDED READING

How To Get Out of Debt, Stay Out of Debt and Live Prosperously
by Jerrold Mundis

The Nine Steps To Financial Freedom
by Suze Orman

Girl, Make Your Money Grow
by Glinda Bridgforth & Gail Perry-Mason

Holy Bible

Live Debt Free
by Ted Carroll

Managing Credit and Debt
by David L. Scott

The Total Money Makeover
by Dave Ramsey

Glossary

Annual Percentage Rate – The cost of credit expressed as an annual percentage of the amount owed. A standardized method of calculation makes the APR useful in comparing the interest cost of different loans.

Bankruptcy - A legal proceeding whereby a person unable to pay his/her debts in full may be discharged from the obligation to do so.

Billing date – On a credit card account, the last date of each month's statement on which transactions are reported.

Chapter 7 Bankruptcy – A process of liquidation of personal or business assets because the person or business cannot pay debts. A trustee is appointed to oversee the sale of all business assets, which are distributed to creditors. Chapter 7 is the most common form of bankruptcy in the U.S.

Chapter 11 Bankruptcy – A reorganization procedure used by businesses, including sole proprietors, partnerships and corporations. The debtor typically acts as his/her own trustee, called a "debtor in possession," and will remain in possession of all estate property.

Chapter 13 Bankruptcy – Allows individuals to undergo financial reorganization supervised by a federal bankruptcy court. Debtors who file Chapter 13 usually desire to pay their creditors but are in financial difficulty. Debtors also usually keep their property but make payment arrangements with creditors.

Collateral – Assets pledged as security for a loan.

Compound Interest – Interest that is calculated on interest from previous periods as well as on principle.

Consumer Credit Counseling Service – A nonprofit organization that provides credit counseling services for individuals and families with serious financial problems.

Credit Agreement – A contract between a borrower and a lender.

Credit Bureau – A private business that gathers and

distributes information regarding credit histories of consumers. Also called credit reporting agency.

Credit History – A statement of the debts and obligations of a person that helps a lender to assess the risk of a loan to that person.

Creditor – A person or business that lends money.

Credit Rating – A creditor's judgment regarding the likelihood you will meet your credit obligations in a timely manner.

Credit Risk – The possibility a loan would not be fully repaid.

Credit Scoring – A mathematical method for measuring someone's credit worthiness according to established relationships among income, outstanding debt, existing credit availability, and so on.

Debit Card – A plastic card that allows you to pay for purchases with funds that are immediately transferred from a financial account.

Debt Consolidation – Replacing several smaller loans that have different maturities and interest rates with a single large loan, generally one that has a longer maturity.

Default – Failure to live up to the terms of a contract

Down Payment – The initial payment on a credit purchase. The down payment reduces a borrowers finance charges and protects a lender's position in the event the borrower defaults.

Due Date – The date on which a load payment is due.

Finance Charge – The total dollar amount paid to use credit. The finance charge includes interest, service and transaction fees, premiums paid for credit life insurance, and so forth.

Fixed Interest Rate – A constant interest rate on a loan.

Grace Period – On a credit statement, the number of days between the billing date and the due date. A longer grace period works to the favor of the borrower.

Home Equity Loan – A loan the uses the equity in your home as collateral.

Installment Loan – A loan with equal periodic payments.

Interest – A periodic charge for the use of credit.

Interest Rate – The cost of borrowing money expressed as a percentage.

Lien – The legal right of a creditor to hold or sell property for payment for a claim.

Line of Credit – The maximum amount of credit a lender will extend to a borrower during a specific period of time.

Maturity Date – The date on which a loan is to be fully repaid.

Minimum Payment – The minimum amount that you must pay (usually monthly) on your account.

Mortgage – A loan to purchase real estate that serves as collateral for the loan.

Net Worth – The value of assets that are owned, reduced by the amount of debts that are owed.

Note – A written promise to pay a specific amount of money on a certain date.

Outstanding – Describing the amount of a loan the remains to be paid.

Prepayment Penalty – The lender's charge for an early payoff of a loan.

Principal – The balance of a debt, excluding interest.

Refinance – Revise a loan's payment schedule to extend payments or reduce interest.

Repossession – A borrower's surrender of an asset when the terms of a loan agreement have not been met.

Rule of 72 – A rule that is a quick and easy way to see how fast it would take your money to grow. Simply divide 72 by the interest you're getting on your money; the resulting number reveals how long (in years) it will take your money to grow.

Secured Credit Card – A credit card secured by funds deposited in a financial institution. Secured cards are designed for individuals who are unable to obtain a regular credit card.

Secured Note – A loan agreement that includes the pledge of an asset that can be claimed by the creditor in the event the borrower fails to meet the terms of the agreement.

Term – The length of time between the signing of a loan agreement and when the loan is to be completely repaid.

Truth in Lending Act – A federal law that requires disclosure of the annual percentage rate and the finance charges on a lending agreement. (Also called Consumer Credit Protection Act)

Unsecured Note – A lending agreement for which no specific assets are pledged by the borrower. The borrower's promise is the only guarantee of repayment.

Usury Laws – State laws regulating interest rates that can be charged by creditors.

Your Credit Report

To file a credit complaint or obtain information about credit issues, visit Federal Trade Commission's Web site at www.ftc.gov or call (877) 382-4357.

EXPERIAN
P.O. Box 9701
Allen, Texas 75013
Security alert call (888) 397-3742
Experian (800) 311-4769
www.experian.com

TRANSUNION
P.O. Box 6790
Fullerton, CA 92834
Fraud alert (800) 680-7289
Disputes (800) 916-8800
Purchase credit report (800) 888-4213
www.transunion.com

EQUIFAX
Equifax information service
Attn: Consumers Correspondence
P.O. Box 740241
Atlanta, GA 30374-0193
(800) 685-1111
www.equifax.com

References

Holy Bible, King James Version

Holy Bible, Joyce Myer's Amplified Bible

Holy Bible, New International Version

United States Census Bureau

The National Association of Realtors

The National Center for Health Statistics; 2001

The National Mental Health Information Center: www.mentalhealth.samhsa.gov

www.moneymatters101.com

www.about.com

Dave Ramsey, "The Total Money Makeover"

Webster's Dictionary

 **MICHELLE TAYLOR** is a Detroit-based entrepreneur and licensed Realtor. She began as an entrepreneur in 1999, when she partnered with a friend to form a real estate investment firm that specialized in buying Detroit-area homes and "flipping" them for profit. A credit repair expert, Michelle is inspired to equip others with the necessary knowledge needed to navigate around the pitfalls of business she found herself in. She is a God-fearing Christian who uses the Bible as her guide to staying out of debt. Michelle believes that biblical principles can guide you in every aspect of your life, whether financial, spiritual, physical or otherwise. Michelle is a single mother of Matthew, and together they live in the Detroit area.

Find out more at TAYLORSWORD.COM

Taylor's Word on
DEBT

How You Got Into Debt...
And How You Can Get Out

MICHELLE TAYLOR

A GUIDE TO GETTING DEBT FREE AND LIVING DEBT FREE

Order Form

To order additional copies of *Taylor's Word on Debt,* please enter the information below and mail It to the specified address.

Number of Books Ordered
@ $9.95 each

x $9.95

Subtotal

$

+

Shipping and Handling
$2.50 per book

$

Total Price
(Subtotal + Shipping and Handling)

$

Name _____

Address _____

City/State/ZIP_____

Make money orders payable to **Michelle Taylor**. Orders will not be filled until payment is received.

Send this form, with payment, to the address at left::

Taylor's Word
P. O. Box 393
Bloomfield, MI 48303

More Than Self Help...

The new *Taylor's Word* Series features powerful and practical tools for living a complete life in many different areas, including

- personal finance
- debt
- parenting
- relationships
- and more!

Instead of skirting difficult issues or offering the same trite advice you would get anywhere else, Michelle Taylor offers *real solutions* to *real issues* that *real people* face.

Find out more at www.TaylorsWord.com